Glimpses of Tynemouth, Cullercoats & Whitley Bay

by

Andrew Clark & George Nairn

Rough Sea, Tynemouth Bathing Pool. 6845

A rough sea crashes over Tynemouth Bathing Pool in the late 1920s. The Plaza is on the right.

Previous page: Whitley Bay Promenade in the 1920s. On the right is a shop advertising 'Pure Whitley Rock – Stamped Right Through.' Behind the shop is Gregg's Cafe.

Also available from Summerhill Books

Glimpses of Old North Shields
by Andrew Clark & George Nairn

Pit Ponies
by Mike Kirkup

Copyright Andrew Clark & George Nairn 2008

First published in 2008 by

Summerhill Books
PO Box 1210
Newcastle-upon-Tyne
NE99 4AH

Email: summerhillbooks@yahoo.co.uk

ISBN: 978-1-906721-02-2

Introduction

This book contains over 100 illustrations that give a glimpse of what life was like in the communities along the coast – Tynemouth, Cullercoats and Whitley Bay.

Tynemouth has its history with the priory, pier and Collingwood Statue. Cullercoats has its bond with the sea and the fishermen, fishwives and lifeboatmen. Whitley Bay has the tourists with the guest houses, Spanish City and promenade. However, what they all have in common is the beautiful coastline that is found north of the Tyne and has been a popular place to live for many years.

Books such as this are a starting point for readers to remember a history that is disappearing very quickly. It is important to recall this heritage and show why Tynemouth, Cullercoats and Whitley Bay are so fondly remembered by so many people.

Andrew Clark & George Nairn
September 2008

A postcard from 1913. Scenes of Whitley Bay and Cullercoats are under a flap on the trunk.

A 1940s advertisement for Welchs, the Tynemouth sweetmaker. The advert proclaims that Welch & Sons: 'now export their Quality Sweets to all parts of the World … it is true to say they are helping to put Tynemouth on the World Map!'

A studio portrait of a Cullercoats fisherman from around 1907.

Tynemouth

Below are three postcard views of Tynemouth from before the First World War. The golden age of the postcard started around 1900 with the introduction of improved printing methods and reduced postal charges. Over 400 million postcards were sent in 1900 and by 1918 that figure had doubled.

Left: Front Street, Tynemouth, around 1912. In the early part of the 20th century, Tynemouth boasted of having one of lowest death-rates in the country. The claim was partly attributed to the abundance of fresh air coming off the North Sea.

Right: Front Street, Tynemouth, around 1909. In the centre of the picture is a branch of North Shields Co-operative Socicty. Now there is a car park in the middle of this wide street.

Left: Percy Gardens, Tynemouth, around 1914. The building of Percy Gardens started in the 1870s and today it remains one of the most impressive streets in the area.

Above: The winding road of the pier approach in the early years of the 20th century.

Right: The Collingwood Monument on Trafalgar Day in 1905. Tyneside-born Lord Collingwood led the fleet at Trafalgar after the death of Nelson.

The canons at the foot of the Collingwood Monument overlooking the River Tyne. In the centre of the picture can be seen the High and Low Lights of North Shields. To the left is the town of South Shields.

Right: 'The Lighthouse, Tynemouth' from a postcard by Robert Johnston. Johnston of Gateshead was a prolific North East postcard photographer from the early 1900s to the late '40s. Each card in his Monarch Series has a unique number and it is possible to date them by this numbering system. Several Monarch postcards appear in this book.

The Lighthouse, Tynemouth. 7054

Left: A view of Tynemouth from the Pier around 1908. The ruins of the Priory can be clearly seen as well as the spire of the Congregational Church.

Right: Soldiers in the grounds of Tynemouth Priory, around 1914. For many years this prominent point was used for the defence of the River Tyne. Now the grounds are used for pleasure with numerous visitors and open air concerts in the summer.

A song from the 19th century celebrated Tynemouth, its Abbey and cliffs:

Oh, the cliffs of old Tynemouth, they're wild and they're sweet,
And dear are the waters that roll at their feet;
And the old ruin'd Abbey, it ne'er shall depart;
'Tis the star of my fancy, the home of my heart …
Oh, give me the cliffs and the wild rolling sea,
The cliffs of old Tynemouth for ever for me.

Auty of Tynemouth

Right: An Auty Series postcard of Northumberland Park sent in 1908.

At the start of the 20th century Messrs Auty Limited, the photographers and photographic publisher, was based at 20 & 21 Front Street, Tynemouth. Their studio, it was claimed, was one of the biggest and best lit in England. They also had workrooms 'devoted to the finishing and touching up of portrait work'. In the days before the average person had a camera a trip to the photographer's studio was where family portraits were taken and developed. As well as portrait photography, the firm was well established as postcard publishers. Matthew Auty, the founder of the firm in the 1880s, was one of the first in the North of England to produce picture postcards from views around the area. An advertisement from around 1900 said: 'Messrs Auty Limited make a speciality of landscape publishing work. They have a large and ever-increasing connection in all the large towns in the North of England extending from Berwick to Harrogate and westwards into Cumberland. In practically every town of importance within these confines "Auty Views" may be had from any good stationer.'

Above: An Auty postcard that was originally published in colour of 'Wreck at Tynemouth', sent in 1905.

Right: The Auty postcard 'Fire at Whitley Bay Free Methodist Church, October 1903.' Incidents such as fires were popular subjects for the postcard photographer.

Tynemouth Sands

Right: A postcard titled 'The Long Sands, Tynemouth' from around 1912 on the far right is the Grand Hotel. Note the childhood favourites shuggyboats and carousel in the foreground.

In the mid 1930s the cost of hiring beach equipment from the Corporation was as follows:

THE LONG SANDS, TYNEMOUTH (736)

Tents for bathers: 4d for adults and 2d for children under 14. *Pleasure tents*: 2/6 for a day; 1/6 from 3 pm to 7 pm. *Deck chairs*: 3d for three hours with a 4d refundable deposit if the chair was returned within the three hours. *Chairs around the bathing pool*: a penny. The charges for the bathing pool were 4d for adults and 2d for children. Swimming costumes and towels could also be hired.

Left: Tynemouth Sands, around 1912.

Right: A family pose for the photographer on Tynemouth Sands in the early 1900s. The ladies are hardly dressed in beach-wear and instead sit on the sand in their long skirts, jackets and hats. Behind the family are bathing machines where visitors would change into their swimming costumes.

Tynemouth Plaza

Right: Tynemouth Palace around 1911.

This well known local landmark was originally opened as the Tynemouth Aquarium and Winter Garden in 1878. The enterprise was not a success and ten years after opening was sold with the Winter Garden becoming a theatre and corrugated iron replacing the glass roof. The building now became the Palace Theatre. There was another overhaul in 1927 and a name change to the Plaza – the name best remembered by local people. In the 1930s

another revamp and a new name – the Gala Land and Ballroom Fantastique. In the postcard on the left the name 'Gala Land' can just be seen on the roof. The packed beach shows how popular North East resorts like Tynemouth were before holidays abroad became the norm. You would need to get to the beach early in the morning to secure a place.

The interior of Tynemouth Palace around 1907.

Above and below: Two views of a beautifully decorated Bazaar that was held in Tynemouth Palace in 1907. On the left in the photograph below is an 'Art Stall' and next to that is a 'Preston & Chirton Stall.'

Cullercoats

Right: Cullercoats from the north, around 1909, showing the small fishing village as it once was. In 1821 a survey showed the village had only 92 houses, 144 families and a population of 536. In comparison North Shields had a population of 8,205; Tynemouth was 9,454 while Whitley had only 1,800 people.

Left: Front Street, Cullercoats around 1909.

Below: The cottages on Front Street in the 1950s, where you could buy fresh seafood from the housewives' doors.

Before the First World War the postcard photographers captured many images of the streets of Cullercoats.

Right: A busy view of John Street with two trams in the distance. On the left is the Cosy Cafe.

Above: Two postcards of the Bank Top with people enjoying the view of the North Sea.

Right: A very quiet Windsor Crescent, around 1912, with no sign of traffic.

Left: Beverley Terrace in the 1920s. This postcard was produced by Robert Johnston in his Monarch Series. Some of his postcards include his bull-nose Morris car which, in this picture, is parked left of the tram.

Above: High Tide at Cullercoats, around 1940. St George's Church, built in the 1880s, is in the distance.

316. FISHERMEN MENDING NETS, CULLERCOATS

Left: Three Cullercoats men carrying on a long tradition of fishing in the village.

Right: A quiet day with only a few people on the beach. On the right is the Dove Marine Laboratory built in 1908. Now part of Newcastle University, it is a centre for field research and teaching.

Right: Three barefoot girls relax on a boat in Cullercoats Bay, around 1914. Behind them two boys have taken a boat out to sea. Cullercoats was a popular destination for visitors and holidaymakers who wanted to take pleasure boats out to sea.

Left: The Harbour, Cullercoats, around 1928. Dozens of bathers are enjoying swimming in the sea while three lads rest on the boat on the left. In those days bathing in the sea was a much more popular pastime than today.

Right: A Johnston postcard titled 'Cullercoats, showing the Marconi Pole' from around 1911. A few years before a Marconi Radio Station had been built and its masts towered over 200 feet. On the right is the Dove Marine Laboratory.

Cullercoats Fishwives

Right: A multi-view postcard of Cullercoats from the late 1930s with two fishwives in the centre.

William S. Garson in his 1935 book *The Romance of Old Tynemouth and Cullercoats* gave this account of the village fishwife:

'The Cullercoats fishwife plays a man's part in helping to launch the lifeboat, frequently wading waist-high into furious and ice-cold waters, and she never hesitates to allow her man to take a place in the boat, even though he may go to face death and disaster. She is hard-working and industrious, clean, civil and intelligent, with an abundance of lively humour and ready wit. Her picturesque fashion peculiar to her clan and which has not changed for over a century, at least, includes a garb of blue flannel, with long shawl entwined about the shoulders, and she carries a creel on her back and a basket on her arm as she travels into the adjoining towns and countryside, singing out:

Share a bonny ling; share a nice fresh cod.
Fresh mak-ker-ril; fresh mak-ker-ril; fresh mak-ker-ril.
Buy crabs, fresh crabs; new-boiled crabs.

A fishwife and cobles at Cullercoats.

'Many years ago, a fleet of herring boats fished out of Cullercoats Bay, and the catches landed there always commanded a better price than the fish landed at any other neighbouring port. When the season was at its height, one would hear the following simple melody, in a tuneful voice, throughout the surrounding districts:

Here's caller har'n,
Here's caller fresh harrin',
Fower a penny caller har'n,
Fower a penny, fower a penny,
Fower a penny caller harrin'.

'Polly Donkin is the best-known and most popular fisherwoman in the North of England. She went to London, at the age of 74, in May 1931, for the first time in her life, and was presented with the Brooch of the Royal National Lifeboat Institution, by the Prince of Wales, for her extraordinary achievements as a collector for the Institution. After doing her ordinary work, meaning tramping of twenty miles per day, as a rule, selling her fish in the country districts, Polly still goes out a-visiting houses and collecting money for various deserving causes.'

Right: Cullercoats fishwives at the station before setting off around the region to sell their wares.

'Many years ago, Ned Corven, a comic singer and an expert violinist, came from the south to join the company of the noted Billy Purvis, whose show was on the New Quay, at North Shields. So impressed was Ned with the Cullercoats fish-lass that he dedicated one of his compositions to her, as follows:

The Cullercoats Fish-Lass

Aa's a Cullercoats fish-lass, se rosy an' free,
Browt up in a cottage just close to the sea;
An' Aa sell fine fresh fish, both to porr an' te rich –
Will you buy, will you buy, will you buy ma fresh fish?

Byeth barefut and bare-legged Aa trudge mony a week
W'i a creel on me back an' a bloom on me cheek;
Aa'll supply ye wi' flat-fish, fine skyet, or fresh ling,
And sometimes penny-wilks, crabs an' lobsters Aa bring.

Aa work hard for me living; fra a friend Aa ne'er begs,
An Aa huff the young gents when they peep at me legs,
Aa's hilthy an' hansom, quite willin' and strang
Te toil for me livin', cryin fish the day lang.

Ned would sing this song to the flare of the oil lamps, the clash of cymbals, and the rolling of the big drum, to a most admiring crowd.'

Waiting for the Boats, Cullercoats Bay.   Auty Series, G.H., N/C., No. 2596.

Left: A group of fishwives on this wonderful Auty series postcard 'Waiting for the Boats in Cullercoats Bay'. The postcard is dated 1905 but it is likely the photograph was taken in the late 19th century.

Lifeboats

A busy day around the Cullercoats Lifeboat Station in the early part of the 20th century. The Lifeboat Station was established in 1852 and its first lifeboat was the *Percy*. The building in this postcard was built in 1896.

In October 1914 the hospital ship *Rohilla* ran ashore off Whitby and so began an epic rescue involving the Tynemouth lifeboat *Henry Vernon*. The *Rohilla* had 229 personnel on board and early attempts by the Whitby lifeboat rescued 41 people. However, local lifeboats were not motor powered and were unable to reach the stricken vessel. Tynemouth's *Henry Vernon* was the closest motor lifeboat to the disaster and set off for Whitby. The lifeboat picked up 51 people and made it safely to shore. Tragically, 84 souls were lost on the hospital ship. Two of the *Henry Vernon's* crew were awarded Gold Medals, the RNLI's Victoria Cross, for their part in the rescue – Major H.E. Burton, boat superintendent, and coxswain Robert Smith of Cullercoats.

A commemorative postcard of the *Henry Vernon* published after the lifeboat saved 51 people from the *Rohilla*. The postcard was printed and published by T. Graham of Union Street, North Shields.

Right: Robert 'Scrapper' Smith, Cullercoats fisherman, wearing the numerous medals he was awarded during his many years service as a lifeboatman. He was awarded two Silver Medals by the RNLI for rescues of the *Dunelm* in 1913 and the *Muristan* in 1916. His Gold Medal came after the brave rescue of the hospital ship *Rohilla*. In 1920 he received the Empire Gallantry Medal from King George V at Buckingham Palace. Robert died in 1927, aged 78.

The Centenary book *Tynemouth 1849-1949* gave this praise to the Cullercoats Lifeboat:

'For speed in launching in emergency, Cullercoats crew have a reputation scarcely ever equalled. In four minutes from the alarm being given they went to the aid of the trawler, *William King*, of North Shields, in 1948. This was an entirely voluntary crew.'

COXSWAIN SMITH V.C. CULLERCOATS LIFEBOAT

F.1517. The Cullercoats Motor Lifeboat "Richard Silver Oliver".

Beken, Cowes. 21303.

Richard Silver Oliver was the first motor lifeboat at Cullercoats. It had only been in service for two years when, on 22nd April 1939, she was overturned while on an exercise. Six people were drowned. A year after the tragedy the *Westmorland* lifeboat replaced the *Richard Silver Oliver* at Cullercoats.

Monkseaton

Above:
Monkseaton
Methodist
Mission Band.
Left to right:
Sidney Varley
(optician in
Whitley Bay),
Jim Hart (local
preacher),
F. Kiy, Ivy Kiy,
Kenneth
McGregor (killed
in Second World
War), Frank Kiy
and Frank
Topping.

Above:
A game of
bowls in
Souter Park
in the
1940s.

Left:
Whitley &
Monkseaton
YMCA Bible
Class in
1926.

Right: The lorry and staff of Gofton Bros, Builders of Monkseaton. A trade directory from 1924 has a Joseph Gofton, joiner, at West Avenue while Richard Gofton, builder, lived in Uplands, Monkseaton.

VIEW OF A PAIR OF VILLAS
ON THE ESTATE.

Left: An artist's impression of a pair of villas on the proposed West Monkseaton Estate. The plan for the estate was to build 300 houses and although the proposal was scaled down there are some villas such as this in the area.

A postcard titled 'A Bit of old Monkseaton', with the Blackhorse public house, around 1925. On the right is a delivery van for Taylor Bros, Meat Purveyors, Monkseaton.

The Brewery in Monkseaton, around 1909. Ale was brewed in the village for centuries until the 1930s when the brewery was demolished.

Whitley Bay

Above: A 1917 postcard of Whitley Road in the Monarch Series by Robert Johnston. Three men with bicycles pose for the photographer and behind them is a steam roller. On the left are two lads – one holding a cricket bat and the other pushing a wheel barrow.

Left: Whitley Road with, on the right, the offices of Whitley and Monkseaton Urban District Council, opened in 1901.

Right: The Esplanade, a street running down to the sea front. On the left is Trinity United Reformed Church. Several of the houses on the right are now guest houses.

Above: The Old Smithy on Front Street shortly before demolition in 1901. Behind the Smithy is the newly-built Council Offices. Next is the Victoria Hotel now a modern pub called 'the bedroom'.

Above: Whitley Road in the early 1900s. Three heavy laden carts are making their way through the village.

Left: St Paul's Parish Church, built in the 1860s, seen here fifty years later. Another heavy laden cart makes its way through the village.

Above: A quiet Ilfracombe Gardens, with newly planted trees lining the street. Today the trees have matured and the street, like all others, is a much busier thoroughfare.

Left: St John's Methodist Church on the corner of Balmoral Gardens and Ilfracombe Gardens. This building was replaced by the present church built in 1922.

Right: St Edward's RC Church, Roxburgh Terrace, in the 1940s. In 1923 a memorial was unveiled in the church to commemorate 17 men from the parish who died in the First World War from the Tyneside Irish Brigade.

Prudhoe Memorial Convalescent Home

Right: The Prudhoe Memorial Convalescent Home in Whitley Bay in the late 1930s.

Potts' Illustrated & Historical Guide of Tynemouth from the late 19th century gives this description of the home:

'The Prudhoe Memorial Convalescent Home, which was opened by the Dowager Duchess of Northumberland on the 14th September 1869, a handsome stone building, in the pavilion style, is surrounded by beautiful grounds, with a fine prospect towards the sea. Here accommodation is provided for 100 male and 40 female patients, who are won back to health and vigour by care and attention, and the healthy breezes from the North Sea.'

In the 1970s the Swimming Pool was built on the site of this famous home.

Left: Staff and residents of the Convalescent Home in the 1930s.

The Women's Dormitory around 1914.

The Dining Hall at Prudhoe Home.

On The Beach

A postcard titled 'Mixed Bathing at Whitley Bay' that recalls a time many years ago when men and women would not always be seen together on the beach.

Above and left: The Children's Paddling Pool, Whitley Bay, in the 1930s.

Historian Anne Dixon recalls swimming in the sea when she was younger:

'How many remember wearing a lovely knitted swimsuit made by your mother or even your grandmother. Remember the feeling when you first went into the sea. Oh my goodness that costume felt like you were in a sack of potatoes with the amount of water it could hold. And how it stretched so that same swimsuit that was made to fit when you were two years old would still be around when you were five.'

Right: A packed beach at Whitley Bay.

Anne Dixon recalls the heyday of the North East seaside resorts:

'There would be rows and rows of tents, all full of families packed together. People hired the tents for the day and

inside you would change into your bathing costume so you could swim in the sea. Others had a windbreak as a protection from the elements and how many remember struggling to put on your swimwear and holding a towel around you at the same time (not easy).'

Left: Youngsters 'plodgin' in the sea off Whitley Bay Sands after the Second World War. A small jetty leads to a boat for pleasure rides along the coast. On the horizon to the right is St Mary's Lighthouse.

The McManners family on Whitley Bay beach in 1952. The boys – James Malcom (Jim Jnr), John Roland and Robert – are with their parents James Edward (Jim Snr) and Winifred.

James, John and Robert McManners on Whitley Bay beach in 1951. The McManners family were from Ferryhill, County Durham and were regular visitors to Whitley Bay in the early 1950s.

Right: Two postcards of the Table Rocks, Whitley Bay, from before the First World War.

A visitors' guide from 1920 gave this description of the Table Rocks:

'Just below the bandstand at the south end of the main Promenade lie the Table Rocks. This spot is a favourite one for those in search of a quiet nook or for those who enjoy painting, sketching or photographing. It is also a good spot for fishing, and enthusiastic anglers may be seen any day keenly enjoying the sport offered. There are many comfortable corners for those who delight to read or to view the wide expanse of ever moving ocean.

An open salt water bath which has been blasted out of solid rock is a considerable attraction for bathers. It is 70 feet long, 5 feet deep at one end and $3^{1}/2$ feet deep at the other, and is covered by the sea at every high tide so that the water never become stale. A number of dressing rooms have recently been erected so that bathers may now disrobe in comfort and thus avoid the predicament many have been in on windy days of emerging from the bath to find their garments in sundry parts of the rocks.

It is not only in the summer time that the attraction exists, for when the storm fiend visits our coast and the sea crashes against the rocks only to be broken into foam and spray and cast harmlessly on the Promenade above, it has a charm unquestionable. Artists of ardent zeal have been known to run considerable risk to secure at this place an impression of the fury of the ocean. Many visitors come specially to Whitley Bay when the coast is storm bound and when all that can be seen for miles and miles seaward are the white crested billows and the foaming ocean.'

Left: The Baths at the Table Rocks, around 1917.

26

Right: The Sands at Whitley Bay, around 1914. Overlooking the sea is Gregg's Colossal Cafe. At this time the cafe had seating for over 1,000 people with 60 windows that faced the sea. There was a special picnic room that could seat 400 and the cafe had its own bakery.

Left: Children with buckets and spades on the Promenade at Whitley Bay around 1910. On the right is the helter skelter. A postcard of the helter skelter from 1907 had this message written by the sender: 'The ride on the mat. Eric always comes back minus the seat of his 'cordeys' where he's been having a ride on it.'

Right: A postcard titled 'The New Promenade Whitley Bay'.

A postcard sent from Whitley Bay before the First World War had this message written on the back:

'Dear Mother and Father. The weather is awful here. It is pouring with rain and the wind is nearly knocking the tent over – but we are happy. We slept in a flooded tent last night. My chest has kept fine so far as the air seems to agree with me.'

The Spanish City

Right: The building of the Dome of the Spanish City with workmen posing for the camera with what looks like few safety precautions. The Dome was officially opened on 14th May 1910. Ten years later a tourist guide gave this description of the Spanish City:

'The permanent buildings comprise a handsome and stately rotunda of a height of 60 feet, the Dome being supported by massive Corinthian columns. A wide and lofty gallery also encircles the rotunda. From this beautiful central hall access is obtained to the new Ballroom which is being altered and entirely redecorated at considerable expense. The grounds are occupied by numerous amusement devices, comprising a Water Chute, Figure Eight Railway, Social Whirl, Joy Wheel, Flying Airships, Hall of Laughter, Maze, Rainbow Wheel, together with a host of side shows.'

A crowd of visitors in front of the Spanish City between the World Wars. On the left is the Cenotaph remembering the fallen of the First World War.

The Water Chute before the First World War.

The Pleasure Gardens, Spanish City, around 1910.

Above: The Ice House at the Pleasure Gardens. The attraction boasts you will pass 'through vast fields of snow & ice.'

Above and below: Two postcards of the Social Whirl Ride from 1909. On the back of the bottom postcard is the message:

'This is one of the greatest attractions at Whitley Bay. I did not venture in myself but it was great fun watching the people that were getting tumbled about.'

A postcard from 1910 showing the Figure Eight Railway ride.

Panama House

A group of children outside the Panama House Cafe, Whitley Bay around 1913.

Steven Fry, the owner of Panama House.

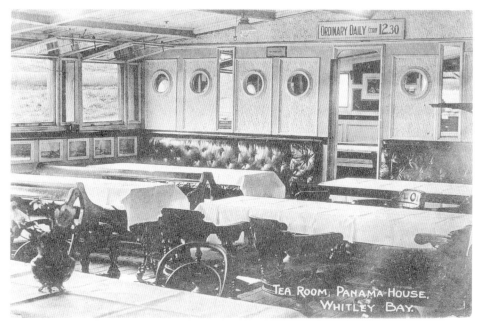

Left: The tea room of Panama House around 1914. This well known cafe was built around 1895 and inside had the look of a ship. Note the port holes at the back of the tea room. Steven Fry died in 1912, however, the cafe he built survived until the Second World War. A fire destroyed the building in March 1945.

Right: Panama House in winter around 1904. The message on the front of the postcard reads: 'Will meet you @ station on Friday. Wish it had been Sat. Rained all day today.' It is interesting to see the use of the '@' symbol a hundred years before its use for emails. In 1904 sending a postcard was as common as sending an email or text is today.

St Mary's Island

Right: An Auty postcard titled 'Old St Mary's Island'. The postcard was sent to Burnhope in County Durham in August 1907, however, the photograph was taken in the 19th century before the lighthouse was built on the island.

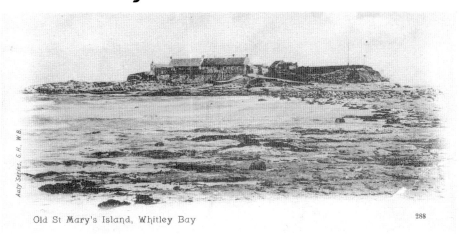

Old St Mary's Island, Whitley Bay

Left: The smoke from a passing boat drifts past the lighthouse on St Mary's Island. The lighthouse was in use from 1898 to 1984. The island and lighthouse are now popular attractions for visitors.

A postcard of a thatched cottage on St Mary's Island sent to Barnard Castle in 1914. For many years the Chrisp family lived on the island.

Transport

Above and below: Two views of Whitley Bay Station, around 1910.

Above: Station Road, Whitley Bay, around 1913. The station, with its landmark clock tower, was built in 1910. That year the Dome of the Spanish City was opened and since then thousands of visitors have used this station to visit the resort.

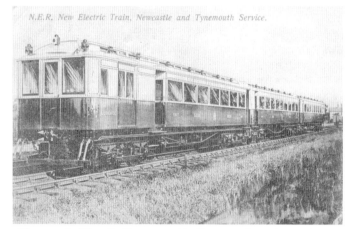

Above: A North Eastern Railway electric train for the Newcastle to Tynemouth Service from 1904. This year had seen the opening of this service and a number of commemorative postcards were produced.

Right: A 1950 advert for the latest in Morris Cars – the Morris Oxford (13.5 hp), Morris Minor (8 hp) and Morris Six (21 hp) – 'the finest cars that Morris ever built'. The cars were available from the main agents – R. Wilson, Cauldwell Lane, Whitley Bay and Coast Road Motor Company, Queen Alexandra Road, North Shields.

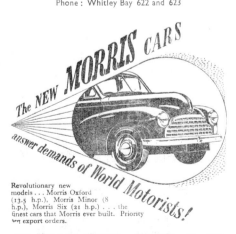

Tynemouth Station

Right: Tynemouth Station, around 1910. On the platform is the T.H. Finlay tobacconist kiosk. An advert on the kiosk says 'El Dronte cigars 3d each or 5 for one shilling.'

A Town Guide from before the First World War gives this description of the station:

THE STATION, TYNEMOUTH. (344)

'As he alights from the train at Tynemouth Station, the visitor might almost be led to believe he had entered a conservatory instead of a railway station, so numerous are the tasteful floral decorations on the platforms. He gets decidedly good impressions, and if unencumbered with luggage, will probably set out for a stroll around the streets.'

Left: Station staff chatting to passengers and posing for the cameraman at Tynemouth Station.

Right: A new electric train in Tynemouth Station.

The historic value of Tynemouth Station has been long recognised and conservation work goes on to preserve it for future generations. Some of the money for this work is met by fundraising by the Friends of Tynemouth Station.

Places To Stay

Right: The Grand Hotel is on the right of this postcard titled 'The Banks, Tynemouth', from around 1913.

At the beginning of the 20th century the proprietor of the Grand and the Bay Hotel in Tynemouth was Mr Tom Tickle. *The Illustrated Guide To Tynemouth* of 1900 had this to say about the Grand:

'The Hotel is a handsome and

THE BANKS, TYNEMOUTH. (737)

commanding structure near the famous Tynemouth Palace and directly on the sea front, enjoying to the full the fresh breezes for which the coast is noted. There is a commodious coffee-room, a handsome and spacious ballroom, a writing-room, and an

Bath Hotel, Tynemouth

admirable billiard-room. The accommodation includes thirty excellent bedrooms and the sanitary provisions are of the best. There is good stabling, and the postal and train arrangements are convenient in the extreme.'

Left: The Bath Hotel, Bath Terrace Tynemouth, in the 1920s.

Houses To Let Furnished

A Guide to Tynemouth in the early 1900s lists the following properties for let:

Address	Rooms Sit'g	Bed	Remarks
5 Percy Street (Sept)	2	6	2 mins from coast, Grand Parade and North Pier, 3 min from trams, 5 from station.
35 Hotspur Street (July to Sept)	2	4	1 min from trams, 4 from trains and Grand Parade. Bath, lavatory, kitchen and scullery.
1 Allandale Place	3	6	1 min from trams and trains, 5 min from coast. Bath, lavatory, kitchen, scullery and butler's pantry, hot and cold water.

Left: Seaham Hotel, South Promenade, Whitley Bay. On the back of this postcard is a map showing where the hotel was located and the following statement:

'A small Hotel having every facility to make your holiday worth while. Adjoins bowling greens, tennis courts, faces sea. Is noted for cleanliness and good cooking. Run under the personal supervision of proprietors Mr and Mrs S.A. Brown.'

Right: The Park Hotel, Tynemouth, around 1950. Today this hotel is still going strong and is a popular venue for functions and weddings.

Below: A comic card showing how busy Whitley Bay could be.

Full up Everywhere at WHITLEY BAY

Above: The Waverley Hotel on The Promenade, Whitley Bay, in the 1930s. The hotel gave an excellent view of the coast and around 1920 was described as having accommodation for 100 guests, lounge, billiard room, large garage, tennis courts and first-class cuisine. Later in the 1920s the hotel was extended and the accommodation was doubled. In 1937 the Waverley became the Rex Hotel – the name it has today.

Entertainment

Left: A postcard of the Corkscrew Stairs with The Empire Cinema at the top. An advert from the 1920s said: 'The Premier Kinema of this District. Super films only shown. If in doubt, ask a resident. They will certainly advise – The Empire.'

Right: Whitley Road with the New Colosseum Picture House showing the 1933 film *East of Fifth Avenue*. The New Colosseum building still stands but has now been converted into shop units.

Left: William Hunter's Pierrots at Tynemouth. Hunter's troupe appeared on the sea front between 1905 and 1908. Pierrots were concert parties often playing in the open air with a collection after the performance. A sign on this stage says 'Seats 2d.'

Right: An advertising card for the Empress Promenade Cafe Concert for Race Week June 1933. On this side of the card is Charles E. Smith – 'The Popular Conductor of the Well-Renowned Empress Symphony Orchestra'. The reverse of the card advertises the other artistes appearing that week, including: Evelyn Copeland 'The Versatile Singing Soubrette' – and Little Muriel Hay 'Another Little Mary Hay'. Other events at the Empress that week included Old Time Dancing, Old and Modern Dances and Whist Drives – 1 shilling or 6d in the balcony.

Charles E. Smith
The Popular Conductor

Of The Well-Renowned

EMPRESS
Symphony Orchestra
WHITLEY BAY

Above: A postcard of Head's Famous Dance Orchestra on stage at the New Empress Ballroom, Whitley Bay.

Priory Theatre
Whitley Bay

NON SIBI SED OMNIBUS

NOT FOR ITSELF BUT ALL

WHITLEY BAY
REPERTORY
COMPANY

Week Commencing 27th March, 1950

Programme Price **3** D.

Above: An advert for Greene's Records of Whitley Bay from 1950. Greene's had shops at Park View and the Exchange Buildings.

Left: A programme for the Whitley Bay Repertory Company at the Priory Theatre from March 1950. The company were performing the play *The Paragon* by Roland and Michael Pertwee.

37

People & Places

Above: Linkletters Patent Shipfittings Co Ltd of North Shields testing out buoyant apparatus on the lake opposite the Plaza before the First World War. The company was formed in 1882 and was located at the top of Hudson Street, North Shields.

Below: A close up of the buoyant seat. Each of these had a capacity for 22 people.

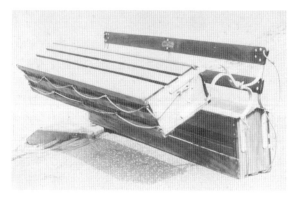

Left: The programme for a meeting of the Tynemouth Abbey Lodge at the Freemason's Hall, Norfolk Street, North Shields on 15th April 1925. The dress code for the meeting was: 'Officers – Evening Dress. Brethren – Dark Morning Dress. All – White Gloves.'

Right: The staff of Evans & Co, the Whitley Bay drapers, ready to go on a picnic on 14th July 1913. The Evans & Co outing was an annual event and the following year the staff went to Morpeth in a motor charabanc.

A horse and cart belonging to the Provincial Laundries of Whitley Bay.

A Hunters' bus outside Woolworth's, Whitley Bay, in the 1950s. Woolworth's now occupies a larger building that replaced its old branch and the former council offices next door.

Right: Whitley Bay FC in 1959. Back row, left to right: H. Ross (trainer), Oakley, Newham, Edgar, Walton, Robson, Browell, Charlie Crowe (manager). Front row: Stoker, Johnson, Duffy, Bell, Mitten. Charlie Crowe moved into management after a successful career with Newcastle United. The highlight of Charlie's playing days was winning the FA Cup with the Magpies in 1951.

The Old Mill at Holywell Dene, near Whitley Bay, around 1912.

Acknowledgements

The authors would like to thank the following who have helped with the publication of this book:

Alan Brett, Harry & Pauline Clark, Charlie Crowe, Anne Dixon, Mike Kirkup, Robert & Stefa McManners, Sharyn Taylor.

Bibliography

Anne Dixon & Andrew Clark, *Durham Bairns*, 2002
William S. Garson, *The Romance of Old Tynemouth and Cullercoats*, 1935
Eric Hollerton, *Images of England: Whitley Bay*, 1999
Eric Hollerton, *Tynemouth in Old Picture Postcards*, 1987
Mike Kirkup, *Charlie Crowe's Newcastle United Scrapbook*, 2001
Charles W. Steel, *Monkseaton and Hillheads*, 2000
Ron Wright, *Cullercoats*, 2002

Guides and Directories

History and Guide to Whitley Bay
Illustrated Guide to the Borough of Tynemouth
Kelly's Directory
Official Guide to Tynemouth
Potts' Illustrated & Historical Guide to Tynemouth
Tynemouth & North Shields Official Guide
Tynemouth 1849-1949
Ward's Directory